PRACTICAL PARENTING

Anne Marie Lee

Practical Parenting

the columba press

First published in 1998 by
the columba press
55a Spruce Avenue, Stillorgan Industrial Park,
Blackrock, Co Dublin

Cover by Bill Bolger
Line drawings by Anna Lee
Origination by The Columba Press
Printed in Ireland by Genprint Ltd, Dublin

ISBN 185607 248 7

Acknowledgements
I want to thank my husband David with whom, and our
daughters Kate and Anna on whom, I sharpened my parenting skills. Thanks to all those who participated in parenting
courses with me over the years and whose shared experience
of parenting their children is found between these covers.
Thanks also for the very valuable work of Michael and Terri
Quinn of Family Caring Trust whose parenting courses I use.

Contents

Introduction

Parenting is the skill of raising children to be healthy, self confident, respectful adults, who are emotionally, psychologically and spiritually well balanced and ready to take their rightful place in society.

It is one of the most responsible tasks any of us will be asked to carry out in our lifetime, yet it is about the only task for which we receive no training. We are somehow expected to know what to do instinctively. But do we?

Most of us manage by basing our parenting skills on the memory of how we were parented as children and by critical observation of the parenting skills of others. We try to avoid the kind of parenting we disliked for ourselves when we were young and often try to make up to our children for the things we lacked. Now this may not be such a bad thing, provided we know why we have chosen a particular line of action and the possible effect it will have on our children.

Parents, in striving to provide the best for their children, often feed into their demands rather than their needs. This can leave children with a false sense of what the world owes them and as teenagers and young adults they will have many disappointments.

Could we be better parents to our children if we studied the actions and reactions we have with them? Would knowing more about our children's needs of respect, encouragement, love, discipline, boundaries, privacy, etc help us to raise them to be better adults?

This book hasn't got all the answers but it will give you a good start on the way to better parenting. Bullying, drugs, alcohol and sexual relationships are not covered here for two reasons, firstly, there is a lot written about these subjects already and secondly, because this book is aimed at the average parent who wishes to stay one step ahead of their child's parenting needs, thereby steering the child away from these problems.

The books contents are based on my experience of parenting for the past seventeen years and of running parenting courses over the past ten years. The situations described are real situations gathered from people over the years and the solutions have been tried and found to work. The advice you find in this book can be adapted to suit your particular circumstances, however, should the opportunity come your way to participate in a parenting course don't let it pass.

Effective Parenting

To parent effectively one must respect the fact that children are human beings with a personality of their own. Children have a need to be treated with respect. By effective parenting you gain the co-operation of the child. The child obeys you out of the love and respect he has for you and because you will show him you are pleased. When you order a child to do something by shouting or threatening him, he is humiliated, he will feel anger and resentment. You can remember incidences like this in your own life! He will obey, but with reluctance and only because he is afraid of you.

When can you start to parent effectively? The day the baby is born. However, if your children are older and you feel they are a little out of hand, it's not too late to start now. Your task will be harder because you have to break old habits to form new ones. *Always remember that you are the best parent for your child.* Don't expect immediate results. Persevere with the changes, one at a time, and you will be amazed at your progress.

Preparing for the new arrival

There is great excitement in anticipation of the birth of a baby, particularly a first baby. You are fully occupied with preparing a room for baby, painting, wallpapering, looking at cots, Moses baskets, prams, clothes, choosing names, etc. Bringing a child into the world is a big responsibility. This child will be in your care and under your guidance for at least the next eighteen years.

Most parents learn the skills of parenting as they go along, drawing on the memory of the parenting they received when they were children. Relatives and friends are always happy to throw in advice too.

Babies needs

The first needs of any baby are physical and emotional security. This security is given in the form of food, warmth and human contact (cuddles). Initially baby cries, feeds and sleeps in whatever order. All the time there is a learning process going on in the baby. She is learning to recognise the sound and smell of first the mother and then of other family members. As baby grows she learns to recognise the family and others by sight. Parents are also learning, becoming familiar with baby and getting to know his or her needs and wants.

Routine

It is at this early stage that you will need to set up a routine for baby so that she will feel secure and you the parents will have some time to yourselves. This is the beginning of effective parenting. Babies who are cuddled sufficiently and are fed and changed at regular intervals during the day are more likely to sleep at night for long periods once they are over six weeks. Babies who are kept up until the parents bed-time are not suddenly going to change their pattern at eighteen months or two years and go to bed at seven so you can be at the cinema for the eight o'clock show.

Communication

When babies cry they are calling for attention but it is the only way they have of communicating in the very early stages. Baby may be cold, hungry, uncomfortable, in need of a nappy change or just bored. She could have a pain from wind. You will eventually get to know the different types of cry which give a clue to what might be wrong. Do check the baby to see what the matter is when she cries.

Often you will see parents and other adults cooing at babies, this is very important. Baby picks up the love and tenderness you have for her in the sound of your voice. Baby will soon begin to repeat the sounds she hears and this is the beginning of language.

Adjusting to Parenthood

While it is very exciting, welcoming a first baby into the family, it brings with it the need for great adjustments to your lifestyle. You may have ideas about how this baby will fit in with your existing lifestyle, but you say this without reckoning on the incredible surge of love you will feel for the baby, and the way this love will cause you to bend to the babies every whimper. You will find it very hard to put the baby down in its cot and walk away if it is crying. There will be days when you are exhausted from night feeds and baby won't settle. You may even feel so low that you are tempted to shake or slap the baby. If you feel like this sometimes, you are not alone, it is quite common. Take the baby to a neighbour, or call in a relative or friend so you can get a couple of hours sleep. Every mother experiences days like this.

Making space for yourselves

Any activities you decide to do must be planned in advance because if you cannot mind the baby someone has to. Gone are the days when you could take up a spontaneous invitation, unless of course, baby is included. It is therefore important that parents make the effort to take time out to spend on themselves, so that their relationship with each other continues to grow and mature.

Forward planning

To parent effectively you need to have given some thought to the ways you will handle situations which might come up in the future with your child. Thinking things out in advance, attending a parenting course or reading will give you ideas which in turn will give you confidence in the decisions you take regarding your child's upbringing. In infancy you will fix a routine within which you will meet your child's needs with love and tenderness but also with firmness. As the child grows and develops language there will be room for discussion regarding choices, consequences and where necessary punishments. As they grow older again and begin to separate a little from you there will be room for reasoning and the shouldering of responsibility. All this in a safe secure background from which the child can explore his surroundings and the world which he will eventually make his own. A background in which he is corrected and guided but not judged or ridiculed.

Time Out for Parents

Most parents become totally absorbed in their new baby. The baby quickly takes over and becomes the hub around which all else turns. Shopping, cooking, cleaning, etc gets done in a rush between feeds and nappy changes. Getting time for a shower or an hour to yourself becomes difficult. What if baby wakes up and cries, or misses me? Some parents feel very vulnerable at this stage and worry about what will happen to this helpless, totally dependant infant if anything fatal should happen to them? All these feelings are quite normal and as you and baby get to know each other you begin to realise the strength of this little infant.

Grandmothers, aunties and friends can change nappies and give a bottle to baby, letting you have an evening out together at least once a week. Start as you hope to continue because if a night out is not part of your routine from the beginning you will find it very hard to go out when baby is older. You may not have the money for entertainment so go for a walk. What is important is the uninterrupted time together. Whether it is mother or father who is the main carer, you need to keep up contact with other adults and make space to develop some interests of your own. The baby needs constant care for the first three years and then he will go to playschool leaving you with time on your hands.

Adjusting to the new lifestyle

Whether you are a single parent or your partner has gone back to work, you may eventually find yourself spending long periods of time alone in the house with the new baby. I believe it is important at this stage for you to find out what activities and facilities are available locally for new parents and babies. Go to the shops for your groceries on a daily basis rather than bulk shopping. This way, if you are known in the area you will meet friends and stop for a chat and if you are new in the area there is a greater chance of meeting new friends. Visit the local park, the library, the health centre and through the grapevine you will hear about parent and toddler groups, child minding facilities, support groups, parenting courses, etc. Of course if you have family living within easy contact and they are supportive you may not need to make use of the local facilities.

You are unique

Because baby takes up so much of your time there is a risk that you may neglect yourself. Make time to have your hair done, keep a little money aside and buy yourself some new article of clothing every now and then. Take an evening class in any subject you are interested in, this will help you to stay in touch with yourself as a unique individual and not to slip into the status of being someone's parent, husband or wife.

Stress

Having a baby is one of the recognised stressors; it is at the top of the list along with moving house and getting married. It brings about major changes in your lifestyle. While you are delighted with the baby and feel overwhelming surges of love for it there are also the sleepless nights, the constant round of feeding and changing. Tiredness sets in and stress levels rise. Once you recognise what's happening you can do something about it. There are many ways of relaxing from taking up a hobby to relaxing with taped music, guided meditations on tape, a hot scented bath, a massage. Getting even a short break from the situation to do something that pleases you will give you renewed energy and enthusiasm for the task of parenting. When you are in good form, rested and relaxed this will have a ripple effect for the good of the whole family.

Babysitters

In order to have time out for yourself and your partner you will need a babysitter. Choosing a babysitter is a big responsibility. Ensure that the person you choose is over fifteen years of age and has a reputation for being sensible and good with children. This information can be obtained by word of mouth. When the babysitter is new to you, have her come and play with the baby one day beforehand. See how she gets on with baby, your intuition will guide you. Give her instructions about feeding, nappy changing, dummies, comforters, sleep patterns, baby alarm and any little personal habits your baby has.

Ensure that your children know the babysitter and are happy with her. Imagine the fright a child would get if he were to wake up before the parents came home to find a strange minder in the house? Always tell your children you are going out and so and so will be minding them, even when you know they will be asleep before the minder arrives.

Make sure the minder has your doctors telephone number and the number at which you can be contacted. It is a good idea to have a back up babysitter in case one is not available and you just have to go out. Babysitters should not be allowed to have friends in while minding your child because this can distract them from the job. Remember, instinct and gut feeling may be all you have to protect your child so if you feel uneasy say no. Treat your baby-sitter well, she is also somebody's child.

Childminders

Good, reliable child minders are worth their weight in gold to you. Handing your child over to a childminder when you are going back to work is a huge tug on the heartstrings for you. I don't know of any parent who found it easy to part with their baby initially. However, I assure you it does get easier, especially when you and your baby grow to know and trust the minder. As soon as the baby is born, if not before, is the time to start looking for your child minder because you will want to spend some time getting used to handing baby over for short periods some weeks in advance of going back to work.

Encouragement Builds Confidence

One of the most precious gifts parents can give to their children is encouragement.

Encouraging

When Lucy comes home and shows you a painting she did in school, stop what you are doing and admire it. Comment on something specific in the painting such as the bird in the tree or the colours she has used. Ask her to tell you about the painting and then suggest putting it on the wall for all to see. It is important to be honest in your praise. Lucy will soon pick up your insincerity or lack of interest if you try to boost her with false praise.

Discouraging

If you had said 'Lucy, your painting is gorgeous! Now go and wash your hands dinner is nearly ready.' Lucy will know that you don't mean what you say and will be discouraged and hurt. If this happens often enough Lucy will stop showing her work to you, just as when you don't listen to her she will gradually stop telling you things. It is so important to keep the lines of communication open with children of all ages.

There is a fine line between encouraging and pushing a child. John's parents, who know John did his best in the school tests, will praise his effort even though they may have hoped for a better result. Karen's parents ignore her improvements if she doesn't come in the top five in the class. Regardless of the child's true ability, John will continue to improve because of his parents encouragement, but Karen will eventually give up trying because she knows she can't live up to her parents expectations. It is desperately important for children to have their parents approval.

From the cradle

Encouragement starts with the baby and continues into adulthood. From praising and clapping when the infant cuts the first tooth and takes the first step, to admiring the teenagers first independent purchase of clothes.

Liam is a perfectly normal, healthy six-year-old. He is the youngest of four and there is a gap of seven years between him and the next child up. Liam's mum dresses him and he has to have his food cut up on the plate or he won't eat it. Liam's behaviour and achievements in school are the same as the other children in his class. At home he is the baby of the family and Liam has learned to play this string to his own best advantage. His parents are not encouraging him to grow and mature. He is their baby.

It is encouraging and confidence building for children when parents give them responsibility according to their age and ability. A bus ride across town to attend a new school may be very daunting for an eleven- or twelve-year-old. However, if a parent takes the trip with him as a trial run, having first got the child to look up the bus map to check the routes and times, his first trip alone won't be so scary. Children should always be encouraged to carry a call-card and to ring home if they are unsure of themselves.

Children can be encouraged from a fairly early age to ring up and make their own enquiries about joining sports clubs, drama groups, art classes, etc. according to their interests, rather than always expecting parents to do it for them. However, I wouldn't push the shy, quiet child, they will do it at their own pace.

Encouraging decision making

Your daughter Maria, aged twelve, needs help with a decision she is trying to make. She is in first year in secondary school, coping well with the new environment. Her teacher wants her to enter with her school to participate in the Dublin Secondary School Girls Choir. Maria is interested but would also like to join the local youth drama group. She cannot do the two because of time constraints, which should she choose? She comes to you for help. While you may have a strong preference for one or the other activity, Maria isn't asking you to choose for her, she is asking you to help her make the choice. Discussion of the pros and cons of each activity are called for, using your superior knowledge and maturity, in the most unbiased way possible, to help Maria make the best choice for her. Dealing with the matter in this way will encourage Maria to be confident in decision making in the future. She also learns, in this exercise, to take responsibility for her decisions. She has made the decision and therefore cannot blame anyone but herself and the decision making process if she is ultimately unhappy with her choice.

Comparisons

Remember each child is unique, so it is not a good idea to compare one child unfavourably with another. It makes the child resentful and angry. Many adults have bad memories of being compared with an older sister or brother at school or at home. As parents we can very easily slip into this habit. It starts when the baby is born. Who does she look like? She looks like herself of course!

Personal achievement

Encourage the child to achieve what he is capable of at each stage for his own sake and not just to please you. Children who are paid for their achievements will learn to work for material rewards. It is not uncommon nowadays to hear of parents bribing their children with promises of money, goods or holidays abroad if they do well in their state exams. These children may not have a good sense of personal achievement and may suffer unnecessary disappointments in life.

Who's achievement

It is important for parents to be self aware when they encourage their children. Are you encouraging your child in a certain pursuit because you recognise the child's talent and potential in this area or are you trying to fulfil a lost dream of your own?

The child who receives appropriate praise and encouragement for efforts made will be confident, independent, decisive and willing to take the necessary risks in life.

Positive Attention

Positive attention is very nourishing. Parents who give regular positive attention to their children are rewarded because their children will be content and secure. They will be less likely to whine and demand, less likely to show off in front of visitors. They will feel valued and respected.

Take some time each day to do things with the children. Some children may be bursting with news when they come home from school. Plan your day so that you can sit and listen to them at this time. Other children may just want to play quietly and unwind after the hustle and bustle of school, and that's OK too.

Cuddles and Hugs

Attention by cuddling is important. We automatically hold and cuddle babies. When they can crawl we get down on the floor and play with them but as they get older we tend to withdraw a bit. Children need lots of cuddles and kisses to thrive. They need to be told they are loved, they are beautiful, etc. and this offering of love must be unconditional. 'I love you just because you are you.' When they hurt themselves they need to be comforted and allowed to cry, this goes for boys too. Take the child on your knee to read a story or watch TV. Don't take it personally if the child doesn't want a cuddle when you offer it. Your timing might not be just right and the child may be too absorbed in something she is doing. Instead, just get down beside her and watch what she is doing, showing you are interested but without interrupting the child's flow of activity.

Using mealtimes

Try and arrange to have at least one meal in the day where the whole family sit at the table together to eat. This helps you all to keep in touch with each other, especially as the children get older. It gives parents an opportunity to hear what's going on for the children in school and at play outside the home, and its also a time where plans can be discussed. The family develops a sense of togetherness and it may very well be one of the valuable memories they will share with their children in the future. As they move into the teen years it becomes more and more difficult to have mealtimes together as they are under pressure to be in different places participating in extra curricular activities. As a family it is a good idea to have at least one meal together at the weekend. This will be at a time when everyone is expected to make an effort to be present. It could be a most pleasant occasion with different family members taking turns to cook. However, if it became an issue to argue over then it would be best to drop it and find another way of keeping in touch with one another.

Time or Money

Children value the time you spend with them far more than the money you spend on them. This is why you will hear adults today complaining that their fathers never took them to the football match, or no one read bedtime stories to them when they were young. It is when you are spending time with them that children are likely to tell you what is troubling them.

When they get to about six years old the children love to have special time out with a parent, on their own. It won't matter much to the child where you go or what you do. Just do your normal shopping at the supermarket and take the child to a cafe afterwards for an ice-cream or soft drink and a chat. Try not to ply the child with specific, closed questions, e.g. 'How was school today?' Answer. 'OK!' 'Did you play with Peter?' Answer. 'No'. To start the conversation ask open questions, e.g. 'What would you like to talk about?' 'Would you like to tell me what made you happy today, or this week?' An open question cannot be answered in one word.

When the child starts telling you her story listen carefully, don't interrupt her or make judgements on what she tells you. If the story gets a bit convoluted ask her to clarify the parts which confuse you. If she tells you things you are not too happy to hear ask her calmly what she thinks of the situation she has just described and gently correct her if necessary. The child will really value this time which is emotionally nourishing for both of you.

Other ways of giving positive attention are to read or tell stories to the children. Allow them to help you doing 'important' jobs around the house. When they are playing quietly its good if you sometimes just sit and watch, don't interrupt them, just watch. They will include you in the game if they want to but whether they do or not they will feel loved by your attentive presence. They will be nourished by the companionable silence that exists between you. You may have experienced this type of attention yourself from other adults.

Spoiling

Parents are afraid of spoiling their children because we all know how obnoxious and selfish a spoiled child can be. To spoil is to 'give in' to a child's demands time and time again. The child learns to expect her demands to be met and when they are not the child reacts badly. Giving your children positive attention when they are not demanding it is not spoiling them, it is respecting and nourishing them. Let them know that they are never too big to be hugged, but do respect their wish for privacy when they don't want their friends to see them being hugged.

Attention-Seeking Behaviour

When children behave in a manner that is rude and irritating to adults they are usually looking for attention. When they seek negative attention some of the feelings they trigger off in you are annoyance, worry, inadequacy and anger. You can change this, not by trying to make the child behave well, but by changing how you respond to the attention seeking behaviour of the child.

Negative Attention

Negative attention is better than no attention for the child. When children are constantly squabbling and fighting among themselves, or they keep coming downstairs after bedtime, even though they've said their prayers and had a story, you feel annoyed and you nag and scold and maybe even slap them. You give them negative attention because they have manipulated you into doing so. You are tired and you want a little bit of space for yourself. All this carry on up and down the stairs leaves you worn out. The children will behave in the same way the next night because you haven't given them any reason not to. The children are not aware that they are attention seeking because this has become their normal bedtime routine. However, they will quickly notice if you change your response to their behaviour.

Using consequences to gain co-operation

With children of three years of age and upwards you can sit down and have a chat about their bedtime routine. Explain that bedtime is not playtime and you want them washed, brushed, prayers said and in bed by a certain time. They can have one story of their choice, allowing a different child to choose each night and then its time to settle down and sleep. Anyone who gets out of bed after that will suffer the consequence of being sent to bed half an hour earlier and of having no story the next night. This is not going to work like magic, its going to take a few nights of you being true to your words before the children realise mum really means what she says. For the first night or two you will find they will behave much as before, so, simply walk them back to their rooms and into bed as calmly as possible and with as little conversation as possible. Don't allow them to engage your attention.

You may have some more suitable consequences in mind for your own children as you know them best. Just be sure the consequences are related to the misbehaviour and not too distant in time from it.

Using choices to gain co-operation

You are in the kitchen cooking, the children are playing a game at the kitchen table when they start to argue with one another. They will look to see if you are paying attention to them. You should ignore the squabbling, interfering only if they are in danger of injuring one another. When the noise gets too much and you begin to feel *annoyed*, *calmly* tell them to play quietly or go to another room. When they ignore you again, open the door and put them out, telling them they can return when they are prepared to play quietly.

This way you give them choices, i.e. to play quietly where they are, or continue the squabbling outside. You do not get involved or take sides. At a later time you might sit and give your full attention to them for twenty minutes or so, doing something they want to do.

When Samantha, aged four or five, won't eat at mealtimes, you get desperately *worried*. Will she become ill? She won't grow and develop if she doesn't eat! You coax, cajole and bribe, you give her the things she likes to eat between meals, sweets, crisps, etc. Samantha is in full control, getting loads of attention. You might even force her to eat by opening her mouth and pushing the food in and she spits and cries and its all very unpleasant. You take her to the doctor who says she is perfectly well and don't worry.

You can change all this by changing your approach to Samantha. Put Samantha's meal on the table. She will pick and poke at it then push it away. 'Are you going to eat your dinner? Samantha' you say in a calm tone of voice. 'No' says Samantha. 'OK I'll take it away then.' Samantha will look at you in amazement, this is not what she expects. She may cry and demand something else to eat, you say 'yes you can have something else after you've eaten what's on your plate.' Don't allow her to involve you in further discussion about it. She will come a little later looking for a snack, you don't say no, instead you say, 'yes you can have something to eat at teatime'. There will be a racket, but you stick to your guns. Don't allow her to go to the fridge or have anyone else give her snacks between meals. You stay calm, she certainly won't die of starvation and by the end of the week she will be eating normally at mealtimes. You have given her a choice, to eat at mealtimes or wait until the next meal. Samantha is no longer getting negative attention for her behaviour around eating. It is important that you give her your full attention for a period of time each day doing something she likes to do. This should be a pleasure for both of you.

You, the parent must sit down and think out in advance, some of the strategies you will use when these kind of situations arise, because, arise they will. Whether you give the child a limited choice or, tell the child what the consequence of a particular action will be, you are allowing the child to maintain his dignity. He can choose to be naughty or good. He will feel he had a part to play in the decision and since children want to be loved they are more likely to choose to be good.

Misbehaviour

Children want to be good, they want to be liked by their peers and by adults. So, why do they misbehave? They do so because they are discouraged, feel inadequate or need attention. Sometimes an accident or thoughtlessness can be mistaken for misbehaviour.

Misbehaviour differs from disobedience in that the later is a calculated and deliberate action usually undertaken by older children. It may occur because parents are too strict, there is poor communication between parents and children, children feel unloved or misunderstood.

Fifteen-year-old Ian was warned by his parents not to 'hang out' with Jack and Peter as they were trouble-makers. Ian tells his parents he is going over to Sara's house for a couple of hours and has primed Sara to tell his parents that he is at her house but just nipped down to the shop for a message, if they call. In fact, Ian has gone out with Peter and Jack, having left instructions with Sara to ring him on his mobile phone if his parents call her house.

Choices and Consequences

Misbehaviour may be dealt with successfully by using

    A. *Choices* – You can do half an hours homework now and have half an hours TV later. No homework, no TV, the choice is yours.

    B. *Consequences* – I will call you once in the morning, if you don't get up you will be late for school and you can deal with teacher yourself. I won't give you a note.

It is very important that you give a punishment that is appropriate to the crime and to the age of the child and that you carry out the punishment. Children are not motivated by empty threats.

Choices

Six-year-old Sally's two cousins came to tea. Sally starts messing her food around the plate and on to the table. This behaviour is unusual for her and may be caused by the fact that Sally feels the two guests are getting more attention than she is. Mum says, 'Sally, either you behave at the table or you go to your room and you can come down and eat by yourself later.' Sally chooses to behave. Mum has used choices before and Sally knows mum means what she says.

Consequences

Ten-year-old Mark was told, more than once, not to play ball in the front garden because he might break a window. So when splintering glass roused Dad from his newspaper, Mark was discovered to be the culprit. Since Mark was older and should have known better his action may be seen as disobedience. Instead of clouting Mark or shouting at him Dad instructed him to get a brush and pan to clean up the glass under supervision. A percentage of Mark's pocket money was docked until the glass was paid for and Mark had to help Dad fix the window. The consequences of Marks misbehaviour lasted several weeks and the message had time to sink in. Dad could have clouted him but very little would have been learned by Mark.

Dealing with misbehaviour in this way is less stressful for you. Helps you to remain in control without losing your temper and is respectful to the child. Children quickly learn that it doesn't pay to misbehave. The child who is given choices will learn to choose the line of action which is of greatest benefit to himself.

He will learn to take responsibility for the consequences of his actions.

The child who is parented by the authoritarian parent, the 'Do as I tell you and don't you dare question me' type, will obey but only because you are bigger than him and he is afraid of you. He will be resentful and angry. When you gain the childs co-operation by using choices and consequences you keep the channels of communication open. The child learns to make good decisions for himself and there is no parent child battle.

Showing off

Showing off is a way of getting attention from relatives or friends. It is a form of misbehaviour. As a parent you mustn't be embarrassed to correct your child in front of others provided you do so calmly and do not belittle or ridicule the child. Where it is possible call the child aside and reprimand her in private.

When the children are young they will question you; 'When can I go on a bus by myself?' 'What age will I have to be before you let me go to town with my friends?' 'Will you let me go to my first disco when I'm thirteen?' It is advisable to anticipate some of these questions and have the answers ready. Your children may try to embarrass you into letting them do things you are not terribly happy about by asking you in front of their friends. If you are indecisive in these matters they will act up and give you a hard time. When they know in advance that your mind is made up and you won't change it, they may feel hard done by but they won't argue too much. In fact, most younger teenagers will be relieved that you are making a stand on their behalf, even though their protocol will demand that they act as if you are the worst parent on the planet.

Accidents

Accidents are not misbehaviour. Small children will spill milk at the table, drop an egg on the floor when putting away the shopping, break a cup or a glass. It will be enormously helpful to the child if you don't over react. Spills can be mopped up and cups and glasses replaced, its not a major disaster. When you react calmly the child does not become frightened and will help you to clean up the mess. When you over react the child will watch with a fearful expression on her face and is quite likely to deny any knowledge of the accident.

Tantrums

Tantrums are usually performed by the 'terrible twos'. They can start as young as eighteen months and continue to the age of four and older if not corrected. There are different causes: tiredness, frustration at not being able to make himself understood and attention seeking. When a child demands sweets in a supermarket and the parent says 'no', child throws a tantrum, kicks, screams, bangs the head on the floor. The other shoppers stop to watch. Parent gets embarrassed and gives in to the child, to stop the tantrum, and get out as quickly as possible. This time it worked for the child so he will do the same the next time. You the parents feel helpless in this situation. How can you handle a tantrum in a public place, with an audience looking on, and at the same time hold your dignity?

Solution

The first time is difficult but, it gets easier. You say 'no, Peter, I'm not buying sweets here. I'll give you something to eat when we get home.' Peter then flies off into his tantrum. The little crowd gathers to watch. You stand by, allowing him to kick and scream, but ready to protect him if he is likely to injure himself. Say nothing until he has spun himself out, then pick him up and give him a hug. In your own way tell him you love him, but that what he did was bold. Remind him that you have something nice for him to eat at home.

Dealing with a tantrum in this way allows you to keep your dignity. To handle the situation your way despite what the onlookers might think. It gives your child the strong message that you are in control, setting boundaries for him and that tantrums won't work in the future.

By hugging him and telling him what he did was bold you are separating him from his actions. You often hear adults saying to a child 'you are very bold' or 'you are a disgrace' when they really mean 'what you did just now was bold' or 'your jeans are a disgrace with all those holes in them'. Young children don't separate themselves from their actions so you must let them know, you love them but not their actions.

Thinking ahead

Parents can prevent tantrums by thinking things out in advance. If you don't let your child see you buying sweets in the shop and you never give your child sweets to eat when you are out shopping then he won't expect them. If, however, you buy sweets and give them to the child in the shop the first couple of times he is with you, then you have set up a pattern and the child will expect to get sweets and when he doesn't you will have tears if not a tantrum on your hands. Save the treats for home. It's no harm to tell grandparents, aunts and others who might take the child out what your rules for the child are.

Avoid situations where you know your child will get overtired. Leave him with a minder when you go to town. A child who is overtired will be cranky and miserable and may throw a tantrum out of frustration.

Tantrums in the older child

Six-year-old Sam started school in September and without much fuss settled in fairly quickly. All went well until he had to have two weeks off school with chickenpox the following January. As he was going back to school his older brother came down with the same illness and was kept home. Although he was quite well again, Sam just wouldn't settle back in school. Every day his mum brought him to school and when she left he cried and screamed, upsetting the other children and the teachers until they phoned her to come and take him home. This went on for five weeks. The parents of the other children in Sam's class complained that he was upsetting their children. The teachers didn't know what to do. The principle thought maybe he should see a psychologist or they should have family therapy. At this point help was sought regarding his parents basic parenting skills. The child's mother and one of the teachers were guided and monitored in the management of the child, at home and in school, for one week.

Sam's mother was very co-operative. She was at the end of her tether, very embarrassed by Sam's behaviour and adamant that he didn't need to see a psychologist. The plan was that mum would hand Sam to the teacher at the school door each morning and he would then have the choice of going to his class and behaving himself while he got on with the class activities or staying with this teacher by himself with nothing to do, no games or books to occupy him so he got bored. He was given a card with faces on it. Teacher was to put a smile on the faces for the times he was good and a scowl for the times he cried. He was not to be allowed out to play after school for the periods of time for which he had scowls on his card, so if he cried at school for half an hour he had half an hour less playtime after school. Sam had the ability to keep screaming and crying for up to four hours at a time.

Each morning after leaving Sam to school mum had half an hours support time to talk out her frustrations and worries about him and to get encouragement and build her self confidence as a parent. As the week went by there was a gradual change in Sam's behaviour. Mum's face began to soften as she relaxed, she was no longer uptight waiting for that morning phonecall asking her to take Sam home as he was too disruptive. She also described how his behaviour began to improve at home because she had learned how to withdraw attention from him when he misbehaved and give him positive attention when he wasn't looking for it.

By the Friday of that week Sam was running in to the school and down to his class immediately. Sam was a success story but 'if he was' his mum was a very concerned and co-operative parent. What Sam needed was to know that the adults in his world were fully in control of the situation and he began to feel secure again once he was no longer able to manipulate them with his tantrums.

 *Pocket Money and Housework*

These two are not necessarily linked, but they can be. The question of pocket money will arise at some stage while the child is in the primary school. The point at which a child learns the value of money is when he is spending what he has earned himself. Some children find it hard to part with their own money but will spend yours without a thought. Other children never seem to have a penny.

Initially children will learn how to handle money under your supervision when you allow them to pay for items you buy at the local shop. Then they begin to spend a little money themselves. They will get presents of money for birthdays, etc and they learn to use this money wisely.

A fixed rate

You may decide to give your child a certain amount of money each week. The amount can be based on what their friends get or on what you feel they should have. Then you must make an agreement with the child about what exactly this money should cover. Is it purely for sweets and treats or is the child to be encouraged to save some and spend some on things he needs as well as things he wants? If he runs out of money in three days what does he do for the other four days? Will pocket money given without expectation of a return build up an expectation in the child of receiving money for nothing in later life? Remember, the child who is given too much will have expectations in adult life that will not be met by society.

Jobs for cash

Another way is to pay for certain jobs around the home and
have the children earn their spending money. This way they can
start earning from a very early age and have some control over
the amount they earn. Again there needs to be discussion about
what you will pay for and what you expect them to pay for. If
your child is to be a conscientious worker in adult life you must
take care that the job you pay him for doing is well done, according to his age and ability. Some children will get the most for the
least return if they can get away with it and they will take this at-
titude into adult life with them.

Choices

If you decide not to give pocket money, earned or otherwise
until the child is eight or ten years old, you could then give the
child the choice of how she wishes to get her spending money.
Give her the option of trying one system for a period of time and
then changing over to a different system until she settles on the
one best for her.

Savings

From the age of seven children can have a post office account
and manage it themselves. Encourage them to save a little of
their spending money towards big items that they want to buy.
Joan and Carmel aged eight and ten got new bicycles for
Christmas. Their mother warned them not to leave them out of
their sight or they would be stolen. One evening the girls came
in for their tea having left the bikes in the front garden. Half an
hour later when they went out to get them, the bikes were gone!
The girls were devastated. The police were contacted but the
bikes were never found. Within weeks the girls were pleading
with their parents for more bikes. They were told that if they got
new bikes they would have to pay half the price themselves. The
girls saved for over a year until they had their share of the
money and the parents put the other half to it for two new bikes.

This time the girls took good care not to have them stolen. It was an excellent lesson for them.

Housework

As a parent you are entitled to some help from the children in the running of the home. It is important to remember though that children are children and they ought not be given more than light chores to do. You are responsible for the running of the home and not the children.

From an early age children can be encouraged to help around the house. It can be a natural follow on from learning to wash, dress and tie shoe laces to tidying up after himself. Helping to tidy his room and learning to make his bed. Taking dishes from the table to the sink or learning to fill and empty the dishwasher.

It is no burden to a child to help with housework provided he is given a fair share to do with his siblings and that what he is asked to do is suitable for his age and ability.

Children will always complain about having to do jobs, the Walton's are the only family I know who do household chores cheerfully. Jobs such as preparing and cleaning up after meals, keeping their own bedrooms tidy and some general cleaning about the house should not be paid for. From the age of ten years on children can make their own school lunches, pack for themselves, under supervision, when going on holidays or weekend camping, etc. They will then be responsible for what they haven't brought and have no one to blame but themselves for it.

Children who contribute to the smooth running of the family in this way have a sense of belonging. They will even fight over a particular job that they regard as theirs if someone else attempts to do it. When the time comes they will be well prepared for life away from home. Consult the children when you are rearranging furniture or redecorating. To include them in such important decisions is very encouraging for them and they realise that you consider their contribution worth while.

Standards of housekeeping are subjective. Some people live in show houses while others live in near chaos. The balance is somewhere in the middle. Home is where you feel comfortable and can relax. Children learn their skills of home making in their primary families.

Manipulative Behaviour

The word manipulation has negative connotations in our society, probably because if the way the concept has been associated with business, politics and advertising. On the one hand you have governments, through manipulative advertising, trying to get parents to have their children vaccinated against various diseases and, on the other hand, businesses are using manipulative advertising to make teenagers believe that their product is the only one which has the power to cure spots and pimples, or to get you to buy one brand of washing powder over another.

To manipulate people is to handle or treat them in such a way and with such skill as to ensure they co-operate with you. The skill of manipulative behaviour can be very good when fairly and conscientiously used, for example, when there is need to correct or chastise children for bad behaviour, instead of beating them physically you use manipulation to get them to co-operate.

Manipulative behaviour can in itself be abusive when it is unfairly used. This abuse occurs when the manipulator uses his skill purely for his own advantage and uses it on those who are in a less powerful position than he, e.g. adult over child, teacher over pupil, manager or employer over employee. In each of these cases the weaker one may lose too much by refusing to co-operate. Manipulation can be very subtle and be wielded by a stronger personality over a weaker one, even when the two people hold the same position or status. It can be successfully used, for a time at least, over someone who is unsuspecting or off guard.

Manipulation is wrong when it reduces or ignores the freedom of choice of its victims.

I don't like to hear a parent say to a nine- or ten-year-old child 'If you're not good all this week you're not going swimming on Saturday'. What does 'good' mean in this instance? For whom is the child to be good – your convenience or his own moral and social development? Will this threat leave the child in a state of anxiety all week, particularly if his swimming session means a lot to him? It's all too vague for the child and come Saturday, if you are off form or tired you may well be tempted to tell him he wasn't good enough and have a lie on in bed instead of taking him swimming.

If your eight-year-old gives you trouble every school morning because he won't make any attempt to dress himself and is slow over his breakfast, keeping you late for work as well as being late for school himself, yet, is up and dressed by eight am on Saturdays because he's going swimming, then, it is quite reasonable to tell him if he can't get up smartly for school and be in time during the week you are not getting up to bring him swimming on Saturday. I suspect you will only have to carry out this threat once and he'll take you seriously after that. In this later case the parent is being very specific and is dealing with one problem which the child understands very well.

You are resisting manipulative behaviour on the part of the child when you stand your ground and manage the tantrum in the supermarket. The onlookers who are clicking their tongues at you are providing the peer pressure, all be it, unconsciously. When children learn to manipulate and they find it works for them, they enjoy using it. It is good to gently suggest alternatives to abusive manipulation when you hear one child say to another 'I'm not playing with you anymore if you don't play skipping with me. The intervention here might be 'Sarah, you want to play skipping!' Sarah, 'Yes but she won't play with me, she wants to play dolls.' 'OK! you have half an hour left to play, I suggest you play skipping for fifteen minutes and dolls for the other fifteen minutes. I'll tell you when it's time to change over.' Children are acutely aware of fairness and are quite likely to co-operate with a compromise like this unless they are very tired and cranky. If they don't co-operate then you might suggest a totally different alternative like 'Right! come inside and you can play dressing up for the last half hour.'

Parents, Keep in touch

The classic manipulation of child is 'Dad, can I stay out 'til ten o'clock tonight?' Dad, 'only if your mother agrees.' Child, 'Mam, Dad says I can stay out 'til ten o'clock tonight!'

The parent peer group manipulates the individual parent into doing things they are not terribly comfortable with. Example: The parents committee arranges a disco for first and second years between your school and the local boys school. It is a fund-raiser for both schools towards their computer funds. There is huge pressure on the youngsters to attend. You feel your child is much too young and immature at thirteen to be allowed go. Both you and your child are being manipulated in the most se-vere way to go against your principles for yourself and your family.

Maybe there is a case for starting local parent support groups. These would allow parents to share their concerns, ideas and principles with other parents. They would be in touch with the current trends in society and in their locality for children and they could support one another in good times and bad. My ex-perience in running parenting courses is that by sharing in the group, parents are taken out of their perceived isolation and are delighted to discover other families are much like their own, the same joys and sorrows, the same battles of will, the same con-cerns.

What you as a parent must be confident of and what you must teach your children is that within the confines of the moral law and the culture within which you live you have free choice. No one can force you to conform to anything which you feel is not in your best interest or that of your family. Now, there may be a consequence involved in taking your stand, but if you have the strength of character to take the stand in the first place you will find allies and the strength to deal with the consequences and you will have held your dignity intact. It is a difficult area and an area which needs to be discussed further.

# The Value of Play

Children learn through play and by copying what they see their parents and other children doing. Parents instinctively teach their children from the day they are born. Parents who play with their children and arrange playtime for their children with other children and spend time choosing toys carefully will find that they are rewarded in the end.

As three-year-old Gavin stands at the kitchen sink playing with plastic cups, mugs and sieve in the water, he is unconsciously learning about volume, quantity, gravity, measurement of space, etc. as he pours from one container to the other.

Children who play with wooden blocks learn to build, they learn colours, numbers and texture. They develop dexterity and fine motor movements, that is, provided that the parent plays with them, encouraging them by praising their efforts and repeating the numbers and colours as they play.

Making a game of it

At first allow Melissa to explore with the bricks. She is fourteen months old. Stand by and see what she will do. First the bricks will go in the mouth, be changed from one hand to the other, looked at, felt, put down, back to the mouth. Then begin to show her how to build. Don't expect too much at first. She will watch what you do and copy. It is important that Melissa has a chance to lead the play. You may show her what you want her to do but she might have a better idea. Whatever she does with the bricks praise her efforts.

Once an activity is turned into a game children will want to play it. So, learning to dress, tie shoe laces, do up buttons or zips, putting shoes on the right feet, etc, all become fun when the child is in good form and full of energy. The child will enjoy showing you what he can do by himself. When the child wants to help with whatever jobs you may be doing, give him something safe and suitable for his age. Praise the child for the effort he makes and don't re-do his job in his presence. For example, if he helps you wash the dishes and they aren't properly done, wash them again but, do it when he is out of the room and busy with another task. Children are very observant and their pride is easily hurt.

Do not do for a child what the child can do for himself except in special circumstances, e.g. tiredness, illness and occasionally for your own convenience.

A kitchen full of toys

From an early age children love to explore among the pots and pans and wooden spoons. As they get older they like to play house under the table or to make a house using upturned kitchen chairs with a blanket or sheet over them. They can produce a much better house from their imagination than any manufacturer of toys could. This kind of play allows children to express themselves creatively and be inventive.

Choosing toys

When choosing toys for children try not to be too influenced by what your friends and neighbours think they should have, or by what other children have. Just because Daragh next door has one of these plastic tractors which he is unable at twelve months old to sit on, doesn't mean that your Mark, who is the same age, should have one too. Buy only a few toys for Mark and the older children but ensure that they are toys they will get play value from. The old reliable toys are still the best, allowing children to use their imagination and initiative, toys like dolls, prams, football, tricycle with trailer, bricks, books, child-sized garden or woodwork tools. With most of these toys the children can play at being adults and that is what they like most of all.

A dressing up box is essential in any house where there are children. This is a box into which you put lengths of cloth and clothes which might be useful for the children to dress up in. Dressing up gives reign to the imagination and keeps children safely occupied for ages, especially when they have friends in.

Not all children's playtime will be educational nor should it be. Children may be encouraged to play for the sake of the pure fun of it. The time when children will feel free to play will pass all too quickly into the phase when they will consider themselves too sophisticated to play. You young parents who have taken the opportunity to sneak a go on the swings or on a slide in the park, holding the baby in your arms as your excuse, will appreciate what I mean. The joy of childhood play never really leaves us.

While television, video and computers have their value and children of today will demand them, I believe we haven't yet learned to use them in moderation. The time some children spend at these machines could be better spent with books, board games and in talking to one another. When children do watch television parents have a responsibility to know that what they are watching is suitable for them.

When your children go to parties in the homes of other children it is your responsibility to know in advance if a video will be shown and satisfy yourself that it is suitable for your child. You may think I'm being too fussy here but I have dealt with children who sat through frightening videos in their friends houses because they were too shy or embarrassed to admit they were afraid and didn't want to be jeered.

Packing up
Many parents complain that at the end of the day they hate to be

faced with a room full of toys scattered on the floor. When children go to playschool there is tidy up time and the children very quickly learn what they must do and they do it willingly. There is no reason why your child couldn't learn about tidy up time around the same time as she learns to make the mess in the first place. It just needs consistence and patience on your part. Help the small child to tidy up by making a game of it. 'I'll put one toy in the box and you put one in.'

Keeping Children Occupied

'Idle hands make devil's work' my grandmother used to say as she ran us out from under her feet to play. There is truth in her statement.

Seven-year-old Ricki is not allowed to go out and play football because its raining. Mum has just cleaned the house so she won't let him play with his Lego in the living room. 'Go and play in your bedroom' she tells him. Ricki is bored. He goes up and sits on his bed staring at the wall. As his eyes rove around the wallpaper he spots a tiny tear where two sheets meet. He pulls it slowly and to his satisfaction a large strip of paper comes off. He begins to look around for more bits to tear off. You can imagine how his mum is going to react when she sees it. Ricki's mum was preoccupied with her housework, maybe she was preparing for guests? We can understand that she needs time to work. Ricki however, was pushed aside when he could have been set up with a job to do that would be helpful and for which he might have been promised a treat, or he could have been encouraged to sit at the kitchen table and paint or do a puzzle which mum could give him an occasional bit of help with. This would have prevented the wallpaper stripping.

Sometimes small children need help to keep themselves occupied. Children of all ages will tell you they are bored, sometimes they really are bored and other times they are simply needing attention.

Planning activities

During the Winter months children are fairly fully occupied in school and there isn't much time to play out in the shorter evenings. During Summer and holiday time more thought has to be put into keeping the children occupied. Plan activities for them in advance of the school holidays. Enroll them in the local summer project, football club, cubs and brownies, swimming club. Be willing, as a parent, to volunteer a few hours each week to support these activities, this helps to keep costs down.

Reading is a wonderful pleasure and educational pastime for children and adults. Enroll them in the library at an early age and give them the habit of frequent visits to it. Most libraries have special activities for children during school holidays. If your child has a special interest or talent encourage it by sending him to classes if you can afford to. Take your children on day trips to the sea or countryside and bring a picnic. Keep your eye on the newspaper for activities which might interest the children and at the same time be free.

Those who have money to spend will have no difficulty occupying children in school holiday time because of all the organised activities which have sprung up to meet the demands of parents where both are working. Care must be taken here not to hand total care of your child over to others, your child needs time with you, his parent. Remember, it is not the money you spend so much as the attention you give to your children that counts.

Making space for yourself

Arrange with a few parents in your local area to take all the children for a day to your house, have a few activities planned in advance to keep them occupied. You will find they would rather think up their own games, this is where the dressing up box will come in handy. Then, in turn, all the parents involved will take the children for a day, giving each parent a few child-free days to look forward to.

Parties

I'm a believer in holding parties at home. As a parent you can have great fun planning a birthday party for one of your children and all your children can help with the preparation. This gives several days of excitement, looking forward to the event. There are several recipe books on the market containing ideas for simple, fun food for children's parties. If you are working full-time then plan the party for the nearest Saturday or Sunday to the birth date. Children will remember these events with fondness in later life. Books on party games for children are also to be found in the bookshops. Older children need to be consulted about the kind of celebration they would like for a birthday and if they prefer a quiet family occasion respect that. The older child might like to help with the preparation and host the party himself with help from you. It is not a good idea for parents to go out and leave their teenager and guests alone in the house. The party can get out of hand or be gate crashed and this can be quite a frightening experience for your child and some of the guests.

Competition

Competition is good for children but it can be destructive if the child experiences too much of it. Treat each child in your family as an individual. While it is time and money saving to have two or three children going to the same club or activity, it may suit one child but not another. If individual children in a family join in different activities to suit their personal taste and talent, they will get a break from competing with one another and have a chance to blossom in their own right.

Taking responsibility

As the children get older encourage them to take up activities in the holidays which will be of educational value to them. They might take on extra classes in subjects they are a bit weak at in school. It would strengthen their sense of responsibility if they

were to volunteer to help with younger children in local pro-
jects, become young leaders in scouts and guides, or train as
First-Aiders in one of the voluntary organisations. These kind of
voluntary situations give teenagers the opportunity to take
some responsibility under supervision and it is a good character
building exercise for them.

Telling Lies and Stealing

This can be a most difficult problem to handle. Children will tell lies if they are afraid of the reactions of the parent or adult in charge of them and may steal to get attention or to highlight a problem they may have.

An accident

Four-year-old Mags is helping mum to put away the shopping. She takes the eggs out of the box to put them in the egg spaces in the fridge but drops one which breaks on the floor. 'Look what you've done, you stupid child' mum shouts, 'now I have to clean up that mess as well as everything else.' Mags begins to cry, from fright and humiliation.

Maybe mum was overtired and stressed but she over-reacted. After all, it was only a broken egg, not a disaster. If this was not the normal reaction for mum, just a once off, then she can apologise to Mags, explaining 'I shouldn't have shouted at you pet, I was tired and you are not stupid, you're my precious and I'm sorry' while giving Mags a hug. Then things will be OK. We are all entitled to fly off the handle occasionally. However, if mum always over-reacts, Mags will learn to lie to her and conceal things from her and from others too, to protect herself.

Children imitate what they see

Children learn more from what you do than from what you say. Dad has often lectured Kevin about lying yet when they sit down to dinner and the phone rings, mum picks it up, 'Hello!

Ah! Joe, how are you?' Dad waves frantically at her, whispering 'Tell him I'm not here.'

Or, a parent rings the boss and says ' I'm not feeling well today I won't go in to work' then goes out to finish building the pigeon coop or goes to the hairdresser or the shops.

Or, the doorbell rings and mum says to John, 'if that's the milk-man tell him I'm not in, I've no money for him this week.' Mind you children have been known to say 'Mam *says* she's not in,' that is until they get the hang of telling lies.

Lies or fantasy

Small children will not understand what it means to lie, they learn to lie. It is said that they reach the age of reason at about seven. Children have lively imaginations and will tell stories as if they are true. They need to be gently taught the difference between reality, fantasy and lying. We tread fine lines between truth and fantasy when we tell children about Santa Claus and the Tooth Fairy. Yet we hold fond memories of these characters right through life.

Children who are discouraged, fearful, lacking in confidence will tell lies if they think it will be the easier way out. They will also tell exaggerated stories to teachers and school mates in the hopes of making a good impression. Children who are confident and sure of the adults around them will tell the truth, taking responsibility for their actions. Confident children will accept a fair punishment for something they have done wrong.

Stealing

Lying and stealing often go hand in hand. A child may lie and not steal but the child who steals must lie to cover up. If you think you are missing money from your purse don't jump to conclusions. Keep an account of what money you have. Check it regularly and keep an eye out to catch the right culprit. Don't make wild accusations as this sets up tension in the family. Don't panic, all you have on your hands is a probable call for help or attention, not a bank robber! Admittedly you will be very upset and worried.

When you are sure who is stealing, take the child aside and have a chat. Listen careful in a non-judgmental way. You want to find out why the child is stealing and correct the problem at source. As with lying, trust is broken and needs to be built up again. This will take time. Give the child small opportunities to show he can be trusted but don't put temptation in his way by leaving money or treats lying about.

Initially the child will be very scared. Punishment may not be appropriate at this stage and more than one chat will be necessary. Take a look at the child's need for money and decide if you are giving her enough or providing sufficient opportunity for her to earn money.

Children often go through a phase of telling lies and or stealing and this will need to be investigated. They may be trying to draw attention to themselves, maybe they are worried about something, being bullied, or feeling unable to cope with some task they are faced with. If there are pressures at home or difficulties between the parents a child might start lying or stealing as a way of coping.

A child who is picked on or scapegoated in the family or in school, always blamed for every misdemeanour, without full and proper investigation, will lie because he is in a no win situation. He is going to be blamed anyway. This is a destructive situation for a child to grow up in.

Breaking a habit

The habit of telling lies is hard to break. It is not unusual to meet adults who have difficulty telling the truth and if you are lied to once you will be suspicious of everything that person tells you. Trust is broken. Both the child and the parent must work on building up trust again over a period of time.

Rebuilding trust

If your child is old enough to understand the difference between truth and lies and you have caught him out in a number of lies, then it's time to do something about it. Approach the child in a calm manner, having first reflected on how you normally react to the child when you catch him out in a lie. Talk to him in his language about how lies are destructive to relationships. Tell him that when he lies to you it is very difficult for you to know whether he is telling the truth or lying. Ask him why he tells lies. Is he afraid of you and the reaction he has come to expect from you when he does something naughty? Encourage him to talk to you about his life, his hopes, his worries, the things that matter to him. By listening carefully and calmly to what he is saying you will come to the bottom of his lying. If his lying is the result of some disturbance or worry in his life it may take more than one session of talking to find the cause and help him to deal with it. If, however, it is because he is afraid of your reactions then you may have to rethink your approach and do a little work on your own spontaneous reactions to him.

May I stress here that if you are going to get good results these chat sessions must be calm and non-threatening to him. He must be allowed and encouraged to have his say without judgment or loss of dignity. You can then proceed to build trust with him and as I've said this will take some time.

 *Dealing With Anger*

Anger is a strong emotion experienced by children and adults when insulted, injured, or frustrated. Anger itself is healthy and good. Many an injustice was righted because someone's anger was raised by the unjust situation. What causes anger to be destructive is when it is expressed in an inappropriate manner, injurious to others, or when it is suppressed causing injury to self.

When you lose your temper you are in a state of uncontrolled or poorly controlled anger. Damien, aged three years, is quite out of control and displays his temper frequently. He asked for something to eat. His mum went to get him a slice of bread, he said he wanted a biscuit. Mum gave him a biscuit. He then climbed up on the kitchen counter. mum lifted him down saying 'You know you are not allowed up there.' Damien shouted at her and kicked her on the shins. Mum put him out in the hall telling him to stay there. Within two minutes he was back. As she put him out again he said he would break something. A short while later a crash was heard. Mum ran out to find the pieces of a glass ornament in Damien's hands and on the floor. Luckily he hadn't cut himself. While all this was going on the two-year-old was watching and absorbing. The mother said that the younger child was beginning to copy Damien.

Expressing anger

Some people have a short fuse by nature while others remain calm, having a placid temperament. Between these two there is a whole range of levels of anger and ways of expressing it. Maybe you as a parent have never stopped to think about how you deal with your own anger. Do you lash out like four-year-old Mags' mum when Mags accidentally drops the egg on the floor as she helped to put away the shopping. Do you remain calm at all costs, suppressing your anger because that's what you've learned to do? Do you acknowledge and own your anger, finding ways to express it constructively, or have you some other way of dealing with it?

Learning to channel anger

Children learn from what they see you do. If there are uncontrolled angry outbursts in the home or long stony, tension filled silences the children will learn that this is the way to express anger. Whether they are the sulky silent type or the volatile outburst type they need to be taught how to express anger in a constructive, non-injurious way.

Encourage the child to talk about the angry feelings and what causes them. This helps them to recognise anger as a normal and often justified emotion and allows them to stand back from the cause of the anger so that they may be a bit more objective in dealing with it. These talks should not be held during or too close to an outburst as the child will be too caught up in the event to think logically or rationally. Some children (I make no distinction here between boys and girls) need to work off anger physically and for these children boxing gloves and a punch bag, or a bean bag to punch, can be a good solution and no one gets injured. When the child talks out the anger and receives sympathy and understanding he might need to cry. this may be the case whether you are dealing with a boy or a girl. Crying releases pent up emotional energy and they will feel the better for it.

Ellen is a moody thirteen-year-old who storms off mid-sentence when you are correcting her. Home is the safest place for Ellen to express her moodiness. Here she receives unconditional love, she knows her parents won't throw her out when she loses her cool. She feels very bad about getting so angry and letting off steam at them but she can't seem to help it. Outside the home she keeps up a front of carefree jollity. Ellen is experiencing the normal emotional turbulence of puberty. At this time she needs lots of understanding and parental support. Firmness is also necessary, there ought to be an invisible line over which she must not step. Giving her space to express her moodiness by banging doors and stomping about the house or lounging in her room is fine, but correction is needed when she back answers or slams a door in your face. She will feel resentful but secure when corrected. Take time out with her occasionally to chat about things.

Taunting

Any child can be taunted by other children but there is a particular pleasure in taunting the child whom you know has a short fuse. Explain to your child that those who tease or taunt only get satisfaction when the one teased loses their temper and reacts. If your child is being teased it is better to teach her to handle it as best she can herself first and see how she gets on. Only if it gets out of hand should you interfere. In this way the child gains in confidence and independence if she has been able to cope by herself with support from you and if she doesn't succeed in coping entirely by herself at least she has tried and should be given praise for her effort. When a child is being teased or taunted and manages not to react, the pent up anger will need to be released at a later time, preferably at home in safety.

If you find yourself constantly going to the aid of a small child who is being beaten up by an older child in the family, stop and take note of the start of the fight. If you didn't see how the fight started don't take sides. Small children can be extremely cruel and clever in the way they taunt an older child knowing they will get away with it because they are smaller and the older child 'should know better'!

Living with Teenagers

When teenagers repeatedly do things which parents find unacceptable, instead of slowly building up a head of steam and then letting fly at them, try letting them know how you feel. You may be surprised at their reaction.

Lack of respect

Every evening Joe and Emma come in from school and drop their bags, sports gear and coats on the floor in the hall. You have told them repeatedly to put away their gear, and they do, for a day or so and then back to square one. Instead of letting this habit irritate you until you explode at them or nag them about it, call them aside and say 'when you two leave your stuff in the hall like this it makes me very angry. I feel you have no respect for me, expecting me to pick up after you. Please put away your things when you come in from school and if you have sports gear to be washed put it in the wash basket.'

You may be making them aware, for the first time that you actually have feelings. If, after a few days you find your plea has fallen on deaf ears tell them again how you feel and add a consequence. 'If you insist on leaving your bags in the hall they will disappear for twenty-four hours and you can make your own excuses to the teachers.'

Thoughtless Behaviour

Joe and Carol go out together every Friday night. They usually have a good time but the one thing that spoils it for them is to come home and find the kitchen in a mess, Their three teenagers and one or two pals watch a video while they are out and then make chips or toasted cheese sandwiches for themselves. Joe and Carol call their own teenagers in for a chat and say 'we don't mind you getting something to eat when we go out but we feel annoyed when we come home to this mess. It spoils our night out. If you cook you are to clean up and leave the kitchen as you found it.'

If they don't improve after the first chat call them in again and tell them once more how their thoughtless behaviour makes you feel. This time add choices, e.g. the next time we come home and find the kitchen in a mess we will call your friends in and tell them how we feel, or, we will ban the use of the kitchen while we are out. The choice will be yours.

Space Invaders

Seventeen-year-old Kevin's girlfriend Natalie comes to his house five out of seven nights in the week. Kevin's mam makes tea and sandwiches for them and they sit in the living room watching telly. Kevin's parents are a bit embarrassed to disturb them so they sit in the kitchen. They feel very put out and upset by this arrangement but they are not sure how to handle it. Natalie seems a nice girl, even if she does seem to enjoy being waited on and Kevin's parents prefer to have him at home rather than out, God knows where.

These parents are allowing Kevin and Natalie to invade their personal space and their home. Its a little bit like when someone stands too close to you and you feel uncomfortable. Kevin's parents need to explain to him how they feel. 'We are fond of Natalie but when she is here we cannot relax in our own living room and this makes us feel resentful and upset. We suggest that Natalie comes here two nights a week. You can have the living room one of those nights and the kitchen the other. If you have difficulty explaining this new arrangement to Natalie we will help you to speak to her.

Margaret's nineteen-year-old son John had moved to Limerick
to study. He shared a house with other students. They had all
modern facilities for washing, drying, cooking, etc yet John arrived home every other week-end with a pile of dirty cloths for
his mother to wash. He entertained his friends in the house, kept
late nights and Margaret was in a sweat cooking for them all,
getting his washing done, dried and ironed for his return. She
began to dread his homecomings until one weekend she con-
fronted him and told him not to bring his washing, she wasn't
going to do it. Two weeks later he arrived with the washing.
'Where are you going with that' asked Margaret. 'But it's dirty'
said John. 'I told you I wasn't going to do it for you, you have a
washing machine and an iron where you live!' 'It was reported
to Margaret at a later stage that John said to his sister, in disgust,
'I'm not bringing my washing home here anymore, she won't do
it for me!' as if it should be an honour for her to do his washing.

Adult to adult

When parents deal with problems by expressing how they feel
rather than constantly nagging and scolding, they show respect
for their teenagers. They treat them adult to adult, without losing sight of the parent child relationship. The teenagers feel the
respect of their parents and their sense of justice is drawn upon.
Teenagers switch off to constant nagging and scolding but, it is
very difficult to switch off when someone starts telling you,
calmly, how they feel about something you are doing which up-
sets them.

Parents who handle problems by expressing to their teenagers
how they feel, are being assertive, owning their own space.

It is very difficult for parents to see their teenagers as separate
individuals with a life and choices of their own to make until
there is some type of physical separation. Teenagers tend to take
parents and home comforts for granted until they are in the position of having to fend for themselves in a flat or shared accom-

modation with friends of similar age. This experience matures them rapidly and they come home at week ends and holiday times to much appreciated home comforts. Those young people who had household chores to do while living at home and who were encouraged to cook, wash, iron, and help with the shopping occasionally, will fare better initially than those who had every hands turn done for them. Their moving out from home will be less traumatic.

Where Are They?

Do you always know where your children are and who they are with? Teenagers are growing into adulthood, they are in a limbo between child and adult and are not sure how they want to be treated. They want to go to discos and hang out with their friends yet they will feel left out and hurt if the nine-year-old gets a treat and they don't. Its not a very comfortable place for them to be, but it is an important stage in the maturation process.

Needing help to say no

Fourteen-year-old Emma came home to her mum and said 'I'm going to ask you a question and I want you to say no' 'OK' says mum, 'what's the question?' 'Can I go to the school disco?' says Emma and mum replies 'no'. Emma had heard her classmates, who had been to discos before, talking about the groping and kissing that would go on between the boys and girls at the disco. She didn't feel she could handle this, she also knew that to say she simply didn't want to go would get her a jeering from her peers. The easiest way out was to say her parents wouldn't let her go, then she could complain about how rotten and uncool her parents were and get the sympathy of her peers. Emma was lucky to have good communication with her parents. She will go to her first disco and enjoy it when she feels ready for that experience, not when she is pressured into it because her peers think its the cool thing to do.

They need you to be in control

While teenagers give an outward impression of having all the answers and being able to cope with any situation, they need to know you are there, in control, in the background. When they go to parties or sleepovers, ring up to find out who is going to be there, what videos will be watched and who is supervising the event. If 'everyone in my class' or 'all the gang are going except me, Mom, you're awful mean.' Ask for names and telephone numbers to ring the parents of 'all the gang' and you'll find that not quite so many are going as your son or daughter would have you believe.

Have courage

Some parents find it very difficult to ring up and check with other parents about what teenagers are up to, but if you want your teenagers to be safe you have to do it, no matter how much they hate it or how uncomfortable you feel doing it.

There is an adult peer pressure which says it is not cool to check up on your teenagers, beware of it! Insist on your children telling you where they are going and with whom. Remind them that if they were sharing a flat with friends and they didn't return when expected from an evening out their friends would also worry about them.

Encouraging hobbies and interests

It is important to encourage any hobbies your your children show interest in or have talent for. The child with a wide range of interests will always be safely occupied but it is up to you the parents to encourage these interests from an early age without pushing. Don't be afraid to allow your boys to pursue what you might think of as girls activities and vice versa. A quiet boy might be much happier at an art class while his sister shows skill on the football field. They will find their own level if they are allowed to explore the options open to them.

When you decide your child is old enough to go into town by himself, ensure he goes with a friend or two and that they have a purpose for going, i.e. to buy books or clothes or to go to the cinema. Put a time limit on them and show an interest in hearing about how they got on when they come home. Don't allow teenagers to hang about aimlessly, boredom sets in and then they get into trouble.

Time limits

Just as there is a time for going to bed when the children are younger, there must be a time for being in at night as they become older. There will always be one who will have a thousand excuses why she had to be a half an hour or more late coming home. Those are the half hours that give parents white hair and stomach ulcers. If they come in after the agreed time then have a consequence such as insisting they be home half an hour earlier the next night. If they are persistently late, ground them for a night. While they are still at school and under eighteen their nights out should be limited, allowing more freedom in the holiday time. Once they get a taste of a social life they may lose interest in study and they haven't the wisdom to know their loss.

The part time job

If they are allowed to work while they are still under eighteen be sure you know where they are working. Accompany them to the interview, it is useful for employers to know that here is a concerned parent. If it is an evening job ensure they have a safe lift home and it is within your time limits. Don't allow them to be pressurised into working longer hours or more days than you feel they can cope with. Ensure that their working environment is suitable for their age and experience and that it is safe. Young people feel they can take on the world but if they over do it in one area another area will suffer. If you see their school work suffering then stop the job. When they are earning money it is advisable to encourage them to spend it responsibly.

With Rights Come Responsibilities

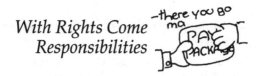

From an early age parents are teaching their children by example, that where they have rights they also have responsibilities. You have a right to your point of view and with that comes a responsibility to respect the point of view of the other person. You have a right to earn money and a responsibility to support yourself and your dependants.

Taking on responsibility gradually

Children grow and mature at very different rates, you only need to look at the first year students in any secondary school. So, children cope with responsibility at different rates also. The ability to cope doesn't necessarily correspond to the age of the child. For example, not every eleven-year-old is mature enough to be allowed into town with a bunch of friends. Fourteen-year-olds can be under a lot of pressure from their peers to go to the local disco, but they may not be ready for it. Some girls are quite mature at fifteen and make competent babysitters, others are not.

From an early age parents can be preparing children to take on these bigger responsibilities by giving them small responsibilities. Firstly they can take on tasks within the house, keeping their rooms tidy, choosing what to wear, taking turns to make decisions about family outings, baking or cooking, mowing the lawn or washing the car, going to the shops with a list, taking a bus ride alone, going to the local cinema with friends during the daytime and so on.

If, as a parent, you feel your child is not mature enough to cope with the situations she might encounter then don't allow her to participate in that particular activity until she is older. She may not understand why she has such old fashioned, horrible parents, but deep down she will feel a lot more secure than if she had been allowed go. If you allow your children to go to a disco at thirteen you can't then stop them from going at fifteen, when, too late, you think they have got in with the wrong crowd. Its much the same with a part-time job. The young person gets used to having money and it is very hard to give that up when you want them to study for exams. It can be a good experience for a teenager to work provided he is encouraged to use his earnings responsibly without taking all the fun out of life.

Adult peer pressure

Adult peer pressure is very much alive. Your child will come in and tell you 'I'm the only one in my class not allowed to go.' This is rarely true. Ring around on a few of the other parents if you are being put under severe pressure and you will find some of them glad of your call because they are under the came pressure from their child. Other parents will laugh at you for being 'over protective' and treat you as though you were a nuisance. These parents haven't the confidence to stand their ground or are so wrapped up in their own lives they don't really care where their children are or what they get up to, so long as no one comes knocking on their doors to complain.

From child to adult

Tom at eighteen is legally of age and thinks he doesn't have to answer to his parents anymore. Tom has just completed a training course and has got a job which pays £80.00 per week. He lives at home where he is the second eldest of five children. He hands up £20.00 per week and thinks he is being generous. For this he has bed and board with laundry done and his share of the bills paid for him.

Towing the line

Tom also thinks he can come and go as he pleases, arriving home at two and three am, then expecting his mother to dig him out of the bed for work in the morning. If Tom was saving a good portion of his income towards a place of his own his parents might be willing to allow this situation to continue for a year or so, provided he was willing to tow the line and keep the house rules. He would be expected to come in at a reasonable hour and contribute to his keep by helping out at home. However, Tom is not saving. His example to the younger members of the family is not good.

Options or choices

Tom's parents need to have a serious chat with him, giving him choices, e.g. reminding him that as an eighteen-year-old and earning he is now responsible for himself. 'We as your parents have done our duty. If you want to continue living here you must contribute £50.00 per week, be home by 11pm on week nights and 1am on Friday and Saturday nights. We expect you to tidy up after yourself and to babysit for us occasionally.'

'Alternately, we will help you to find a place of your own and give you items of furniture and kitchenware for it. You will pay your own rent, electricity, telephone, food and clothing bills. You can then come and go as you please and live according to your own standards. Should you choose this option and it doesn't work, you are welcome to come home again, but, on the terms we have spelled out. Or, maybe you have another option in mind!'

Is it fair?

You may think Tom's parents are being unreasonable in their demands. If they allow him to continue behaving as he is he will have the unrealistic expectation that life and society owe him something. When these expectations are not met he will be disappointed. With a greater sense of his right to take than of his responsibility to give, he will probably be unhappy in marriage too. This same example could apply to a daughter as easily as to a son.

If you feel isolated in the task of parenting older children why not get a Parents Support Group going in your area or participate in a Teen Parenting Course.

Privacy

Privacy regarding nakedness is fairly strongly developed in children by the time they are three years old. A two-year-old will quite happily sit on his potty in the kitchen and jump up, delighted with his achievement, to the expected praise of his parent. The presence of other people probably won't bother him. By the time they get to five and six some children will want to lock the bathroom door. The need for privacy will differ with different children in the same family, some will be quite precocious while others are self conscious and shy. The wishes of the children in this matter should be respected, it is not a good idea to make fun of them.

Encouraging children to communicate

Depending on the needs of the child and the reactions of the parents children will be more or less open in sharing information. Some children will come home and in their innocence will tell tales on themselves. Mark comes home from school and tells you that he was put at a desk by himself because he was talking. You can react in several ways, three of which are:

1. You will listen to the tale calmly, acknowledging that your son was being disruptive in class and annoying the teacher by talking. Teacher solved the problem by separating him from his classmates. In this case Mark will come home and tell on himself again and will have confidence in your ability to listen to him.

Or

2. You will reprimand your son all over again for his disruptive

behaviour. In this instance Mark will learn to keep things from you.

Or

3. You will become quite indignant that the teacher would have the gall to make a show of your son in front of the class. This kind of reaction gives Mark an inflated sense of his own importance and undermines the authority of the teacher.

If young children find they can communicate easily with their parents and that no topic is barred then as teenagers and young adults they will continue to discuss issues with you. If you have built up this kind of openness between you and your children, you can be sure that as they communicate with you, your children are taking on board your values and comparing them with the values of the peergroup, values which are not yet fully formed. As the children get older confidentiality will be most important. They won't be happy to hear you repeating their conversations with your relations or friends. You need to know what they consider to be private for them and seek their permission to share that information with others.

Openness in communication

It is essential to keep the lines of communication open with your children at all times. Therefore your reaction to what they tell you is important. If you over-react they will close up. Keep a spirit of openness in the family, encouraging the children to share with you information about what is going on for them. Be prepared to share a certain amount of information about yourself with them.

Without crowding them take an interest in what they are reading and watching on TV, be interested in their friends and the conversations they have with one another. Don't open your children's post but encourage them to be open about the letters they receive. There is a fine line between being interested and prying. If you pry children will close up. Unless you have very good reason for doing so it is not a good idea to go through your children's rooms, cupboards, dressing tables. Teenage children need privacy, if they are lucky enough to have a bedroom of their own then siblings should show them the respect of knocking before entering and asking permission to go into that bedroom if necessary when the owner is not there. When teenagers share a bedroom it may be a good idea for each one to have a cupboard or chest of drawers which is private to them alone. This means of course that they are responsible for keeping their space clean.

Should you notice a *major* change in your child's behaviour and a change in her circle of friends which disturbs you, then you must deal with that situation as you see fit. You may want to seek professional advice before you make your move because, while parents are seldom wrong in their suspicions, there may be a temporary breakdown in trust which will be difficult to heal.

When children reach puberty it is good to mark the occasion with a celebration, after all this is an important milestone in the child's life; the threshold of the next stage in human development. Children tend to be shy and awkward about the changes that are happening to them at puberty and one would want to be sensitive in ones approach to them. Around this time they are moody, unsure of themselves, think a lot and discuss with their peer group. They will need more personal space, and they seem to spend a lot more time sleeping, which we parents might be inclined to interpret as laziness.

Until your son or daughter is eighteen you should know where they are and have set times for their return home. If they are in the habit of telling you where they are going and with whom, they will probably continue this as long as they live at home. On the other hand they may need to exercise their independence a bit more and should be allowed to do so within reason. When they bring their friends in give them space to 'do their own thing' within reason. You may be happier to have them in your home and know what they are up to.

Parents need privacy

Parents also need privacy especially when there are growing children in the house. The children need to be taught from an early age to respect the privacy of each other and their parents by knocking on bedroom doors before entering. Many parents give children the habit of coming into their bed in the morning. This is a habit they often come to regret and find hard to break. As children get older they should be encouraged to take more responsibility for themselves. Parents can be slaves to their children and never have time for themselves, if this happens they have only themselves to blame. Parents are entitled to privacy in the home, to sit and read the paper or engage in a hobby without interruption.

Children's Spiritual and Moral Development

Morality

The word morality may immediately conjure up in our minds something to do with sex. Morality is about distinguishing right from wrong, good from bad, so that we might live in harmony with the other inhabitants on this planet. Children must learn the moral codes of behaviour of the society in which they live. These moral codes are linked in with culture and are different from one society to the next and at different times in history. So we don't kill or injure each other indiscriminately, we try to be polite to one another, we are allowed one wife or one husband at a time, we are expected to obey the rules of the road, the school rules and various other rules of society, and to remain sober.

Spirituality

Spirituality is how we live our lives in relationship with God, with people and with our environment. One doesn't have to practice institutional religion to be moral or spiritual, but it helps if you do. If you do practice a particular religion it will have a set of laws which you will be expected to obey and pass on to your children.

What children take on board

While you are raising your children you are consciously and unconsciously passing on to them the moral and spiritual codes by which you live. This happens because of your children's tendency to observe and copy both what you do and what you say. If you smoke and drink alcohol in front of your children there is little point in instructing them not to smoke and drink. Have you ever heard a parent admonish a child for swearing and a few sentences later swearing himself? If you are the type of person who always looks for good things to say about other people, especially about the children your own children are having difficulty with, they will learn to look for the good in others too. When you are kind and caring towards your sick or elderly neighbours, when you give what you can to the poor, etc your children are observing and absorbing.

This spiritual dimension is what draws us to seek meaning in existence. It is the dimension which draws us to seek personal space, to be quiet, to meditate and to search. Although people search for the fulfilment of this spiritual dimension in all sorts of places, it is actually to be found within oneself. The spiritual dimension in children needs to be acknowledged and nourished, some will do this through religious practice and others will find other ways, e.g. by observing the wonder of nature, through art, music, philosophy, science, philanthropy, etc. It is through nourishing our spiritual needs that we come towards peace, contentment and fulfilment, therefore it is important to attend to the spiritual needs of our children.

The value of reflection

In the busy, noisy, fast moving world in which we live, parents must make a point of creating quiet, reflective spaces for children. When you can, take them into the countryside for walks, or to the seaside to listen to the waves lapping against the shore. Turn off the TV and let them read books or read to them, provide them with the materials to paint pictures, plant seeds in the garden and so on. If you celebrate religious festivals give your children a sense of the true meaning of the festival. Explain to them the religious history behind the festival so they don't get totally wrapped up in the commercial exploitation of it. Give children the habit of saying some short prayers at bedtime. At meal times say a prayer of thanksgiving for the food and for all those who helped to bring it to the table from the farmer to the cook.

Ritual

Ritual is important in helping children come to terms with powerful emotions, it helps them to process grief, anger, sadness etc. When the goldfish dies there may be a need for a funeral rite and burial service. They can wrap the dead fish in tissue and put it in a box to be buried in the garden. Time can be spent making up a poem to be written on card for the headstone and a jamjar of flowers won't go amiss. The tears expressed in this ritual can help to process emotions that have very little to do with the actual death of the fish. While some children will take this type of ritual very seriously and benefit from it for others it will simply be a game to be played and thought no more of. These experiences in childhood are a healthy preparation for adult life.

When they go wrong

As we have discussed in other chapters children who lack confidence and self esteem or who are afraid of reprisals will steal and lie to boost their confidence and defend themselves. If they are not getting the love and attention they need at home or from the extended family they will seek it, possibly in negative ways, outside the home from friends and school mates. If the parents are too busy to be aware of where their children are, who they are with and what they are up to the children can drift into bad company and trouble. Morally and spiritually they will feel bad about themselves and will begin to feel a sense of despair about their own ability to achieve something better in life. This downward spiralling process can be reversed once the child finds someone who believes in him, be it a parent, teacher, relative or friend whom he respects and who is willing to give time to the child. The child will learn to live by a more acceptable moral code and feel good about himself.

Religious practice

If you are a family who practice religion and for whom this is important you will be very upset when your children question your beliefs and rebel against your practices. This is a time for great patience and a willingness to listen nonjudgmentally. Young people often need to discard the beliefs and mores handed down to them by their parents in order to consciously take them on board again but as their own free choice. Be assured that if you have given them a good basis on which to build their adult lives they will find a level which will be quite acceptable to you.

The Physically Disabled Child

The physically disabled child is one who is disadvantaged by such conditions as asthma, diabetes, deafness, speech impediments, paralysis – from needing to use walking aids to being wheelchair bound – and many more. We seem to have a strong instinct to protect or cosset the disabled child from the hiccups of life. In truth, this child needs to be tougher than the average child to survive and lead a happy fulfilled life. If the body can't be toughened the spirit can. Disabled children's psychological, emotional and spiritual needs are the same as the able-bodied child. they have the same tendency to naughtiness, selfishness, moodiness and goodness as their siblings and friends. If their demands are constantly met out of sympathy they will become as obnoxious as any other spoiled child.

Pamela was a pretty six-year-old who wore callipers on both legs and propelled herself along at great speed with the aid of crutches. Unfortunately Pamela was spoiled by the adults in her life: her parents, relatives, teachers and hospital staff. She was bright and talented but had difficulty relating to other children because of her selfishness and unfairness in playing games with them. What would this child be like at sixteen? I suspect she will be angry and embittered, feeling life has dealt her a raw deal. The adults in her childhood fulfilled her demands but her teen peers will find her to be a 'pain' and they will avoid her.

Getting the balance

Parents are usually very anxious that their child will go to regular schools rather than special schools so that they might mix and grow with and have as normal a life as other children. The trap they can fall into is in treating their disabled child too differently from her siblings at home and expecting too many concessions at school.

Philip was a thin, pale ten-year-old who had a fairly severe form of asthma. He was one of six children but got an unfair proportion of the attention of his parents and the other children felt it. Philip had his own dust free room while the other children doubled up. He didn't play games out doors and when he came out he was well wrapped up, even in Summer. If he didn't get immediate attention when he called for it he'd have an 'attack' and then everyone ran to him. He missed a lot of school, more because he didn't like school and manipulated his way out of it than that he was too ill to go. When Philip grew up his brothers and sisters had no time for him, they resented him. He eventually got married but his marriage broke down. He had become so self-centred he could only relate to people on his own terms. He tried to manipulate the adults around him as he had manipulated his parents but they weren't having it.

Children with disabilities don't want to be treated differently. Encourage them to lead normal lives but don't deny that they have some special needs, instead, help them to come to terms with this fact. Encourage them to mix with other children who have the same or similar disability and with whom they may feel a certain solidarity. If your child is going to a regular school this may mean joining a specific association dealing with her type of disability. In this way she will be comfortable socialising in all types of company and have the added opportunity of keeping in touch with up to date information about her condition. If the child goes to a special school try to ensure he gets opportunities to mix with able-bodied children by joining clubs or activities outside school. Many adults feel awkward when introduced to a blind, deaf or wheelchair bound person, they are at a loss for something to say This wouldn't happen if there was more mixed education and socialisation in childhood; they would learn to be comfortable with one another.

Let them experiment

Let your disabled child do all he can for himself. Let him experiment with public transport, going out with his friends to town, the cinema, etc. in the same way as you let his siblings experiment when the time is right. Your son may very well give you heart attacks when you see him doing 'wheelies' in his chair and you think he'll tip over and split his skull. But, your daughter could also give you heart attacks when she is out on her skateboard or bicycle. Skill in these activities give them self esteem among their peers and help them to discover their own limitations. You can make them as safe as possible by insisting they wear helmets and knee and elbow pads but don't stop them because of your fears.

A fair share of attention

When you have a disabled child it is particularly important for you parents to take time out individually and together. Continuously monitor the situation, with the help of someone outside the family if necessary, to ensure you are not focusing in on this one child to the detriment of the rest of the family. While the whole family acknowledges the special needs of this one child and all are encouraged to help, they too have needs which must be met. While some disabilities dictate a dependant lifestyle for the future adult, other children require training for future independence. One of the disabling factors can be an over anxious parent who is unwilling or unable to let go. Treat the disabled child the same as your other children where possible, encouraging and correcting, setting boundaries and letting go. Use the same parenting skills for all your children.

Puberty

Puberty is a very special time for young people. It is a new experience for them and for you their parents. You could have several children in the family and each one might experience and deal with the milestone of puberty differently. Any difficulties they may experience may arise from the fact that they don't really know what to expect and are unable to express these new and often turbulent feelings they are having. Parents should not allow themselves to be influenced by the horror stories others will tell them of how difficult teenagers will be at this time. Remember this is your child, the one whose tantrums you coped with, whose joys you shared and whose griefs and sorrows you smoothed over. If you expect trouble it may oblige you!

Puberty is a time for celebration. A shedding of childhood to take on adolescence. It is a gradual process in which the child will vacillate back and forth from adolescence to childhood until she feels comfortable in adolescence. Children develop more quickly now than in the past. It may be necessary to begin talking to your child regarding what to expect at about the age of ten. Again, you know your child better than anyone else and must make the judgement about how much information to give at this time. Talk to your child with the aid of a book if necessary, but do talk to the child, don't just produce a book and say 'its time you read this.'

Becoming comfortable with the task
Think back on your own experience. How were you told? Did you find out for yourself? Were you ashamed, shy or embar-

rassed by what you were told or by the discomfort of the person telling you? Many parents express their discomfort at the prospect of facing such an intimate conversation with their own child. If you feel like this maybe you could discuss with a friend what you intend to tell your child and in this way become more comfortable about it. Recently parents have been saying that their children are asking questions after watching advertisements for sanitary protection on television. Questions must be answered!

Use proper names for body parts when talking to your child. This gives the child a language with which to talk about sex in a loving context and also to describe events more accurately should they find themselves in the unhappy position of having to do so to the authorities, in cases of abuse.

Coping with physical changes

Major physical changes take place in both boys and girls at puberty. The boys may be gangly and awkward in their movements and mortally embarrassed if you tease them when the voice starts breaking. They will anxiously peer into the mirror looking for the first signs of facial hair and will need lots of assurance if there is any delay in its appearance. The girls will either be confident, even precocious, wanting to wear garments which will show off the first signs of budding breasts or, they will be shy, hiding themselves in extra large tee-shirts and jumpers. Talk to the girls about periods and to the boys about wet dreams so that they won't be shocked or frightened when it happens to them. Even in this day and age I've known children who thought they were bleeding to death or dying of cancer because they had been unprepared. Take on board the fact that you, the parent, are responsible for passing this information on to your children, unless you make a definite arrangement for the school or other authority to do it for you. Whichever way your children handle this process, they are depending on your support, encouragement and understanding to get them through.

Practical points

During puberty the body begins to perspire more. Adolescents become aware of the need to use deodorants and perfumed body sprays. Encourage the use of deodorants rather than antiperspirants. Some young people need lots of encouragement to take baths and showers while others hold up the bathroom for hours, to the annoyance of other family members. Buy cotton socks for malodorous feet and supply open sandals for use around the house.

Lounging around the house and sleeping late at weekends and holiday times seems to be the norm for most young people at this stage. I believe they need this rest and they need time to think about life and the problems of the world. However, it is also important to keep them focused on something they are interested in as well as on their schoolwork.

Spots and pimples can be a preoccupation with those who have oily skin. The pimples will stay until they go, no amount of special creams or ointments will vanish them away. If there is a family history of spots and pimples then the children are more likely to get them. Blackheads can be kept at bay and pimples reduced considerably with careful washing, using soap and water with a little lemon juice or vinegar added to the water. Pimples that are picked may leave scars. The earlier they appear, sometimes as young as nine years, the earlier they will disappear.

Protecting you children

Society no longer has a chaperone system to protect its females. Parents have a responsibility to protect their children, sons and daughters, until they are at least eighteen years old. This means talking to both boys and girls about respecting each other; about coping with sexual feelings and urges until they are mature enough to take responsibility for their expression within a loving, long term relationship; about the rights of babies and children to have the love and attention of two parents who can provide the security they deserve (financial security is only one aspect and not absolutely essential) Parents have a responsibility to ensure that while their daughters may follow the latest fashion, they dress in a way that is not sexually provocative.

Groups

Young people are safer in groups at this age. If you open your house to their friends you will know where your own are and can supervise them all. The peer pressure will be very strong to have a boy or girl friend. The individual child will not be ready for this and will need support to 'have a life' which doesn't include exclusive relationships with the opposite sex.

A mentor

If the child can have a mentor or confidant, e.g. an adult friend of the family or a relative who is a good listener, this can be very helpful. The child can bounce ideas off the mentor before approaching the parents if they are unsure how the parents will react. The mentor will, hopefully, be a mature person who will guide the young person safely, challenging any gravely unacceptable behaviour. This is not a relationship you can introduce your adolescent to after you read this. It is a relationship which must be built up over a number of years.

Bed Wetting

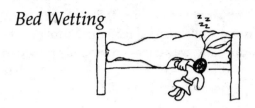

If there is a history of bed wetting on either side of the family the risk of one or more of your children bed wetting is increased. I would not be prepared to say that a child wets the bed because he is lazy. A parent's belief that a child is lazy can be reinforced when the child remains dry while staying overnight at a relative's or friend's house. However, if the parent is allowed to believe in the child's laziness, it only leads to further tension in the family and deterioration in the relationship between parent and child.

Conor, at eight years of age wets the bed five or six nights out of the seven. It didn't bother him until lately. Children who bed wet often think they are the only one with the problem and that there is something radically wrong with them. Now he is more aware of his problem because he has the opportunity of a weekend away with the cubs but he doesn't want any of his friends or the cub leaders to know he wets the bed. What is he to do? His mum doesn't nag or scold him about it as she knows Conor is not lazy and would love to be dry at night. She has a lot of extra work to do, washing Conor's bed linen and keeping odours at bay, ensuring his siblings don't jeer him or use his problem against him in arguments and boosting his confidence in areas that he is good at. Conor's mum was a bed-wetter herself so she understands the problem very well.

Conor was never dry at night but had no problem during the day. His mum kept him in nappies at night until he was four and then decided that it wasn't good for his ego to wear nappies

when his three-year-old sister didn't wear them. Instead she
protected the bed with waterproof sheeting and got a waterproof cover for his duvet. Conor takes a shower every day to
keep fresh and to protect his skin from getting sore. He is perfectly dry during the day, this is an indication that there is nothing radically wrong with his urinary system.

Some Causes of Bed Wetting

Apart from a family history of bed wetting in the otherwise
healthy child, other causes can be :

A chronic urinary tract infection.

A high anxiety level in the child.

Fear of the dark.

Forgetting to use the toilet before bed.

A deep sleeper.

Drinking too much just before bedtime.

Tips for training

Ensure the child gets ten hours sleep per night.

He must empty his bladder before bed and again before
going to sleep if he reads for a while.

No more than one hour of supervised television per day.

As many drinks as he wants during the day but no drinks
after the evening meal.

No fizzy drinks at all.

It can help to lift the child and walk him to the toilet about
two hours after he falls asleep. Stay with him as he might
sleep walk.

Set the alarm for seven in the morning and see that the child
goes out to the toilet.

Don't use nappies on children of four years or older, it is not
good for their self esteem.

Protect the bed with waterproof sheeting.

Steep the bed linen and pyjamas as soon as possible to reduce
odour.

The child should take a shower.

By keeping these rules you may be able to keep the child dry and when he gets used to a dry bed the very action of wetting in his sleep will wake him up. The vast majority of children who bed wet will grow out of it around puberty but many will be cured earlier by patience and training.

If you have a child who suddenly starts wetting the bed having previously been dry then you need to look for a cause. The cause will be anything from an infection to stress caused by some problem the child has in school or at home which she is unable to cope with or talk about. Stress caused by parents fighting or talking of separating, a new baby coming, school exams, quite a common one is the stress caused by the preparation for First Communion. In such cases the anxiety involved shows itself in bed wetting. Once the stress is removed the wetting will stop.

Daytime wetting

Suzy is seven and is constantly wetting her pants during the day. She has no problem at night. Even though the other children tease her about it and her skin is often sore she still won't come in and go to the toilet in time. Suzie knows when she wants to empty her bladder but gets too absorbed in her games to come in and use the toilet. When she does come in she is hopping from one leg to the other and bursting 'to go'. She wets herself in school too because at breaktime she is too busy to go to the toilet.

Day time wetting is a problem with many children usually under ten. It is not necessarily connected with bed wetting. It may be caused by an infection and will clear up when the infection is successfully treated. Most of these children wet because although they have the sensation that the bladder is full and needs emptying, they are too absorbed in what they are doing to answer the call of nature. They might need to take extra clothing to school in case of an accident there, teacher will need to be informed. There is no point in nagging and giving out to the child because this will have no effect on the child other than to damage her confidence and make her feel got at. The child needs practical help and is not able to help herself.

Some Tips:

See to it that the child goes to the toilet and empties the bladder before school.

Speak to teacher and she will ensure the child goes to the toilet at break times.

The child can go to the toilet on coming in from school and at roughly two hourly intervals until she goes to bed.

Be aware that some children will run to the bathroom when instructed to do so but will simply stand there for a minute or so and not actually use the toilet.

Regular showers are necessary for children who wet by night or day to prevent rashes and soreness.

Results

When the child has a few consecutive dry days or nights you will notice a difference in their self confidence. They will be delighted with themselves and this is proof enough that no child wants to be different from his peers.

Other Childhood Problems

Nightmares

Children of two, three and four years commonly have nightmares. They will wake up in the night obviously frightened and needing reassurance. This may be because they are taking in an incredible amount of information which they are unable to process or express verbally. This period passes as the child's language improves. It is for this reason that it is so important to supervise the child's television and video watching.

Older children can have nightmares if they are exposed to horror films or ghost stories. Nightmares can also occur when the child has an infection, this is different from delirium, caused by high temperature and which occurs while the child is awake.

Some Tips:

Supervise your child's television and reading material.

Advise him to come home when the other children are telling horror stories.

Leave a low watt light on in his room or on the corridor with the door open at night.

Reassure the child and distract him with healthy stories.

Never ridicule or laugh at a child's fears. To the child these fears are very real.

Nail Biting

A nasty habit. It is unpleasant to watch someone biting their nails. It is a habit that usually begins in childhood and can often carry on into adulthood. Children who start biting their nails can be of a nervous disposition but not necessarily so. They will bite their nails when they are anxious or under stress. It is a very difficult habit to give up.

Some Tips:

Encourage the child to stop biting the nails on the two little fingers first. When these nails are reasonably long add the next two fingers and so on until all the nails except the thumb nails are long. When the child is ready she will stop biting the thumb nails also.

It can help if you give the child something to fiddle with instead of nail biting, e.g. worry beads or a piece of paper to fold.

It is probably better to get the child's co-operation in giving up the habit rather than force her by using unpleasant tasting nail paint.

Bad Language

Small children will pick up and use bad language without realising that it is offensive. The reason is often because when they first use bad words they get a reaction of surprise and laughter from the adults who hear them. The child may get this reaction the first few times she uses bad language until the adults realise 'this has gone too far' and they change their reaction to one of reprimand and punishment. The child is then surprised and confused and will either stop using the bad language or will use it all the more to get revenge on the adult who – in the child's eyes – was nasty to her.

Clare, aged four years, was standing on a chair at the kitchen sink playing with a basin of water and some plastic dishes. Mum heard her say, with some exasperation 'Oh! s—t!' and looked up to see that Clare had spilled some water on the floor. 'Clare, what did I hear you say?' Clare turns round and says 'I said s—t

Mummy.' 'That's not a very nice word' mum says calmly. 'But
you say that when you drop things' said Clare. 'That's true
Clare, but it is not nice is it? So if you hear me saying it again will
you remind me that I shouldn't say it.'

If you don't want your child using bad language you mustn't
use it yourself.

Speech

Some children up to the age of about five years may begin to
stammer. They rapidly repeat a word or syllable to hold the attention of the listener until they think of the rest of the sentence.
If the child has been speaking normally and suddenly begins to
do this then you need to look at a few things.

   What kind of attention do you normally give the child when
   he is talking to you? If you can give full attention the child
   will be able to take his time telling his story.

   Don't comment on the child's manner of speaking, just listen
   and respond.

   If you are busy and cannot listen just when the child wants to
   talk, tell him so and arrange to listen at a later time but don't
   forget to do so.

Children at this age are unable to express clearly and quickly
what they want to say. The stammer is a way of holding your attention until they can put words on their story. However, if
there is a family history of speech impediments you may need to
have the child assessed by a professional. The less fuss or notice
is taken of the child when he stammers the better. Some children, if they find that the parent will sit them down and make a
fuss of listening to them because of their stammer, will continue
to stammer in order to get the attention. There is a fine line between allowing the child to manipulate and giving the necessary
attention.

Older children form bad habits of inserting 'gap fillers' such as 'ye see,' 'ye know what I mean,' 'De ya get me,' 'Em, em, em,' and lots or others. These are inserted frequently between sentences and are not relevant to the conversation at all. They can be very irritating for the listener. Gently pointing them out can be enough to get the child working on dropping them.

Soothers

Also known as doodies, and dummies. There is rarely any need to give these to babies but unfortunately it is very difficult to convince parents of this fact. They are a source of infection because no matter how careful you are the soother will be dropped on the floor and replaced in the child's mouth without being washed. They can effect the older child's ability to form words clearly especially if the child is allowed to talk with the soother in its mouth. Try putting a pencil or pen between your front teeth and saying a few sentences! If the child sucks a soother after twelve months of age there is a danger that the front teeth will be pulled forward by it.

If you feel you need to give a soother to your baby because he is very fractious then only give it when absolutely necessary and for a short period of time. Don't have your beautiful child looking permanently like Maggie Simpson. Babies shouldn't be allowed to use a bottle as a soother either. Transfer your baby to a cup at twelve months if not a little before.

Julie wouldn't part with her soother at four years old. Her mother was very anxious about getting rid of it and wanted her to give it to Santa Claus. Julie only sucked it in the house and never in front of her friends. The advice Julie's mum was given was to let her have it at night but remove it from her mouth when she fell asleep. Mum had introduced her to it and hadn't removed it before twelve months, there was no point in traumatising the child by forcefully removing it now.

A Word to Grandparents

Grandparents are a most valuable asset to any child. They are the magical people who tell stories, give treats, have time to listen, support and comfort and of whom the grandchild will have a store of happy memories. They are so valuable that many parents will seek out surrogate grandparents for their children when their biological grandparents are dead or living too far away for regular contact. Children get their sense of family history and heritage from grandparents, they acquire a sense of identity from them.

Grandparents rights

I'm reliably told that grandparents have rights. The right to enjoy and cherish their grandchildren. The right not to be taken for granted. The right to say no to child minding proposals. The right to be paid for child minding. The right to be respected by their grandchildren. The right to hand over parenting responsibilities to their sons and daughters. I would encourage you to come up with any other rights you think appropriate.

As your son or daughter is gradually adjusting to parenthood you must gradually adjust to grandparenthood. It is a very different role from parent and needs to be reflected on if you are to be happy in it. Initially there may be a few hiccups as the roles cross over and you will feel hurt when you are told, 'She is my child, I think you should ask me before giving sweets to her!' If you have two or three children think ahead and don't give more to the first grandchild in terms of time and goods, than you feel you can afford to give to subsequent grandchildren, whom you haven't yet met. There can be great jealousy when one grand-child appears to get more attention than another in the same family or among cousins.

When grandchildren come along grandparents can offer a lot of support to the young family but, it may be wise to hold back on the advice unless it is asked for. Young parents often resent grandparents 'interfering'. In the last two or three generations styles of parenting have changed drastically. The rules by which you raised your children may not be the same rules by which your children will raise theirs. Give praise where you can and avoid criticising. Your son or daughter may be struggling with this new role and their confidence easily shaken. However, you have the right to expect your grandchildren to live by your rules when they come to visit you.

At home Liam has his dinner handed to him on a tray each evening and he eats it in the front room watching television. At his Gran's he sits at the kitchen table to eat and there is conversa-tion during the meal. Liam prefers to eat at his Gran's.

Three generations living together

Problems can arise when a daughter has a baby and comes home to live with her parents. The young mother is no longer a child living at home. She is now a young adult, parenting her own child. This requires considerable adjustment on the part of mother and grandmother. The daughter may never have lived independently of her primary family and adjustments which would have been made had she lived in a flat and fended for herself have now to be made within the family circle. If the young mother is under eighteen she will need boundaries, guid-ance and support from her parents. Encouragement to continue in education would be of benefit to her for her future prospects of employment and independence. The young mother must pay a realistic contribution from her income towards her upkeep and that of the baby and should be expected to respect the rules

of her parents as long as she lives in their home. She must nego-
tiate with her family for babysitting and child minding services.
Grandparents must keep in mind the fact that their daughter is
the parent of this baby and has the right to decide on the style of
parenting she wants to follow.

Enjoy grandparenting

For grandparents there is wonderful opportunity to enjoy
grandchildren without the responsibility of parenting them.
You can have them to visit or stay over and hand them back at
the end of the visit. You can enjoy their company and teach them
things you didn't have time to teach your own children.
Children keep you young especially if you enjoy good health
and take time to spend with them.